Words on Stony Ground

Poems inspired by Life, Loss & Love

Sue McFarlane

FIRST EDITION

Published in 2024 by

GREEN CAT BOOKS
19 St Christopher's Way
Pride Park
Derby
DE24 8JY

www.green-cat.shop

Dedication

For Alex, always

Contents

Acknowledgements

Many thanks to my many friends and family members for all their continued encouragement and support.

Sincere gratitude goes to those who have trusted me to put together appropriate words for some very specific projects. I have been humbled many times.

Appreciation to Morgan Gleave for his fabulous artwork between the little informal sections of this book.

For her unstinting attention to detail and chivvying up, cheers to Lisa Greener, my publisher at Green Cat Books.

Much love to Alex for his unending support and for boosting my morale. He also found and took the fantastic photo for the cover of this book.

So many people have helped with the compilation of this, my third volume of poetry.
I thank you all, you know who you are.

Introduction

Since my other books, "My Words for Living" and "Travel Safely Within" were published, words have continued to arrive; via pen, pencil, keyboard and dreams, never really stopping. The actual poems sometimes faltered but a steady stream of ideas washed into my consciousness and held forth, waiting to be written down and shared.

I have been very fortunate in making new contacts and enjoying many memorable poetry opportunities.

There have been poetry workshops, both supporting others in their writing but also for me to develop my own skills. Live poetry readings at Open Mic sessions as well as the Nottingham Poetry and Newark Book Festivals have led to working with other artists. A major exhibition in aid of the National Holocaust Museum carried a poem I was invited to pen to accompany a bespoke artwork. A local business approached me to contribute poetry to their remembrance multi-media presentation also working with a local veterans' charity.

I have poetry included in an anthology (First Flight) compiled by an accomplished writer, Leanne Moden, who leads the Paper Cranes Poetry Group. It was there that I have met many other great poets including Laura Grevel.

My inspiration continues to be from many sources. This collection is a genuine mix of topics, emotional responses and calls to action. Each poem has a story within its form, of which there are again new variants as I experiment and develop as a poet.

As the reader, you are invited to try them all. Please say the words out loud if that helps you to interpret them in your way. Find the beginning, middle and end to each story. Although the meanings might change along with your energy levels and mood, each time you turn the pages, I trust that you will find some new favourites amongst "Words on Stony Ground".

I am forever grateful to you for supporting me and my poetry.

Words on Stony Ground

Poems inspired by Life, Loss & Love

1

Foreword by Christine Riley

If you are asked to write a foreword does it come as a surprise? Is it something 'other people' do?

It can be a bit intimidating, daunting even but ultimately it has to be a fantastic privilege and honour. A chance to praise and critique in a way that would not be part of day to day conversation with a friend.

Quite different characters that somehow gelled, Sue and I are well matched; I enjoy reading poetry and Sue enjoys writing. As a friend who has shared laughter, pain, fear and the odd tear, I feel so privileged to be able to put down in words the admiration and happiness I feel, knowing Sue. From meeting at dance classes, walking during the pandemic to sharing dreams and fears over pot painting, our friendship has deepened. That does not mean we are sycophantic, no, quite the opposite as we do question as well as praise each other but always trying to encourage better habits and skills.

When one has a gift to create it is often compelling, rightly so, to share what you have produced so that others can also enjoy. Some are gifted the ability to create scenes on canvas, swirling paint and crayon to create scenes that capture a moment in time, others craft beautiful melodies or cacophonies – like all things artistic it depends on your taste. As a poet, Sue shares her verse with us so we may be transported, in our minds, to a wide variety of situations, some more poignant than others. The Christmas tree poem was one such offering that hit me harder than one would think but is, perhaps, analogous with the challenges of war and other situations, where not being the best enables survival for another day. There are too many poems to comment on individually but I can see that being involved with the Holocaust Museum gave rise to emotions that found their release in words on many pages. However, it is not all doom and gloom! There are many lines celebrating love, family and life in general. Allow the sunshine offered in these to penetrate your psyche and your heart.

Since the first book 'Words for Living', a collection of poems recording experiences during Covid difficulties, Sue has been prolific. The new poems show a developing confidence and maturity of dialogue, confirming both her ability and increasing understanding and assurance in producing poetry, using many different techniques and styles – you may find some more to your liking than others but that's ok, read and enjoy or move on.

Practice makes perfect and the continuing flow of poetic verse that Sue has managed during the last few years, has enabled her to create this third volume for our perusal and pleasure. I know she is proud of this achievement but equally proud, as she should be, of performances, guiding others and being commissioned to write poems around topics concerned with the Second World War, praise indeed for her writing talents. I know this was as emotionally draining as it was challenging but perseverance paid off and both the Holocaust Museum and local organisations have had their repertoires enriched by Sue's contribution. I can also see the impact coming through in other poems not about war.

Hopefully, once started with this book, you will read and reread all the poems. Like music and food our tastes change, sometimes over time, sometimes more rapidly as a life event changes our perspective or mood. A particular favourite of mine is "Now". Very sage advice but how many of us, having read it and maybe even silently agreed, will reflect and follow the guidance?

Poetry

Words there on blank page

tell a full, vivid story.

Take time to wonder.

New Chapter

A door closes shut,

Another new life chapter

Begins, grows, expands.

Now

Just be in the moment,
This moment,
Not time that has passed,
Remembered, or
Even a minute into the future.

Right now, be in the present,
Your present.

Breathe and allow your lungs to
Fill with life-giving air.
Catch the coolness of it
Now.

Taste those sensations in your mouth,
On your tongue.
Notice them all
Now.

Hear the many sounds
All around you,
Signalling to you,
Actually being here
Now.

Smell the atmosphere,
Full of scent particles,
Strange chemicals,
Real only for a short time
Now.

See by opening wide your eyes and
Your soul-being to the universe.
There is so much more that you could
Capture from this moment now,
Right now.

This moment passes on to the next;
The present tense in the present sense.

Live for your now,
It is all there really is.

Imbolc

Frost crisps the ground,
As the blood red sun claws its way up
Above the horizon,
Its fingers pointing accusingly into the day,
Out and towards the west.

Skeletal tree silhouettes in the light,
Black against the russet
Colouring the clouds.

Warmth slowly permeates the air,
Misty and fresh.

Sunlight creeping across the ground,
Bare now but full of nature's promise.

Windows are full of fire,
Reflecting arched golden light.

Spring

Rise, waken, alight

Green shoots, energy abound

Push up out beyond.

Plant

Plant a seed into the soil,
Await its glory.
Tender shoots breaking the crust,
With green life anew.

Plant an idea in your heart,
A new thought.
Allow it to flourish and grow.
Soon you will bring joy to many.

Plant a kiss on their cheek,
Show love and care.
They will remember it always,
Feeling warmth deep inside their heart.

Morning Care

Cosseted under a thick duvet, which
Embraces and warms your tired body,
Away from bright light of a new day
And the icy blasts of spring.

After a fresh cold water spritz,
Turn your wrinkled sleep-deprived face
Into a flexible pillowed smile,
With magic scented soothing lotion.

The muffled cosy sounds change
To clear wild staccato cries.
No longer snuggling, cocooned,
Your baby is wide awake,
Needing you always.

Snowdrops

Hanging heads down low,

White blooms fringed with lacy green,

Snowdrops welcome spring.

Storm

Leaden clouds shifting
Across a purple, bruised sky.

Vengeful tide, roguishly delinquent,
Heaving nonsense
Over shores of discontent.

Deep sea spoils leaving
A blemish on virgin sand.

One Foot in the Grave

Torn down in wild storms,
Wrenched by winds,
Waging war against the wooded copse,
Found in the aftermath.
An epic living being,
Linking earth to sky.

Holding onto sharp rocks,
Burrowing roots deep.

Stalwart, defiant, undefeated.

This tree might be broken but
It will not be beaten.

Higher up the sculpted trunk,
Lying aground,
New growth evolves,
Showing strong, new green fists
To the world.

Inspired by a fallen but not dead tree, seen on a visit to
Hestercombe Gardens, Somerset.
Dedicated to Carole Speed.

In the Air

Spring is now in the air, we can feel it.

Spring is the time for a new beginning, take it.

Spring is full of green unfurling, you can see it.

Spring is trees full of blossom, can you smell it?

Spring is so much warmer than winter, welcome it.

Spring is plants alive with the buzz of bees, you should hear it.

Spring is such a wonderful season, do enjoy it.

Magnolia Holding On

On a cold but bright spring morning
I opened my slender petals wide.
The sun shone and distilled their aroma,
Stars bright against a true blue sky.

No leaves yet to shelter my blossom,
The strong wind has blown away many.
Frost came and bit off my petals,
Rains heavy took ever more plenty.

Today there is only one flower left
Holding on to a tender stem, tight
But my buds are now filling out nicely
And my lush leaves will soon be a sight.

The Rose

Nestling in the leaves, a tiny bud is hidden.
As days go by, filling out and growing,
Sunshine and showers, dark earth feeding,
Coming to fullness as sepals begin to open.
The sharpness of thorns protects a juicy green heart,
A parting of armour shows the first temptation of colour.

A rosebud now shows on the long, strong stem,
Petals unfurling as they greet the light.
Colour deeper at the centre, with a tangible pallor,
To surrounding petals laced within each other.

A bloom opens fully, with petals out wide,
A simple climber or hybrid tea.
No matter if you cannot see this beauty,
You pick up its scent on a mild summer breeze.

Ruffles at the edges created by rain showers,
Makes for an untidy but still eye-catching flower to
behold.
The perfume intensifies in the sun, under clear skies.
Bees and butterflies visit, rest a moment, feeding.

As the days pass by, the blossom shrivels and dies.
A haw now obvious, with its seeds hidden inside.
The next generation is secured as this ripens,
A fabulous red fruit attracts birds to their supper.

The earth is then blessed with the remains of the rose,
But the circle of life is determined and fulfilled.
Our needs, when young, met by parents and elders.
We come into our own, live our life and blossom,
Passing on the mantle to others in our prime,
Before letting descendants follow on from us,
As we reach our own end.

*Inspired with thoughts that along with the huge sensory
overload of perfume & variety of colours, roses have
beauty through the whole of their bloom life.
Live life to the full, through all your years.
Appreciate those around you, wherever they are in their
wisdom & goodness.*

Holiday Lines

A love story in print, contrasting with the page,
Depleting volume behind the edge as it's avidly read.
Adjustable but still uncomfortable, sunbed's frame
afoot,
White stone balcony balustrade cutting through the
view.

Shadow lines growing through the day as the hot sun
shifts.
A weathered lounging space now damp with salty
spray.
Harsh, glossy metal safety railings at each cliff level,
Mason hewn stones contrast with the deep, clear sea.

Ropes of bobbing buoys securing bathing space,
Waves swell, lined up, meeting the harshness of rocks.
Yellow and orange kayaks paddled frantically but full of
fun,
Swell of frothy spume follow on from snarling jet skis.
The shallow wake in the surf after varnished wood
ferries.

A rocky shore far off, with coves and small sandy bays,
The skyline etched in columns of green Cypress trees.
Jet streams follow incoming traveller jets across the
blue sky,
But the ever-changing clouds, no lines could attempt to
define.

Inspired in Dubrovnik by the view from the terrace.

Dawn

Dawn bleeds with sunlight,

Horizon scarred, clearly lined.

Night becomes new day.

Menorcan Shade

Wind pruned leafy glade,

Providing much welcome shade.

Sadly our last day.

Cut Flowers

I have a small posy of flowers
Hand-picked between rain showers.
My friend chose them today
And brought them my way,
As a gift from the special place
That always, brings a smile to her face.

Summer

Coloured blooms perfume

Verdant pastures, heady days.

Abundant sunlight.

A Rose by Another Name

As deep Autumn Colour blooms,

The Ebb-tide of this year looms.

Hot Chocolate promises to warm

A Peacemaker for the heart within.

Just take one Moment in Time,

Sit quietly,

Breathe deeply,

Be still.

Inspired by names of scented rose in the Castle
Garden, Colchester.

Sweet Dreams

Rows of trimmed purple blooms
In Provence, baked in dry heat.

Bees buzzing around our heads,
Their pollen-drenched bellies
Full of aromatic, sweet nectar.

Harvest now lush and ready,
Plucking stems slowly pressing in hand.
Perfume released, provocatively heady.

Oil extracts, knowingly medicinal,
An ancient herb to soothe and calm.

Now dusk on this balmy summer evening,
Sun setting and calm descends.

Grecian Blues

Blue Aegean Sea
White windy tidal tops
Blue painted church roofs
White walls bright
Blue tinted water glasses
White chunky china cups
Blue volcanic stone sills
White pristine tablecloths
Blue cat-scratched doors

Blue evil eyes everywhere
White contrasts in all light
Blue azure acrylic skies
White scanty, billowy clouds
Blue cold water bottle tops
White bleached beach timber
Blue tiled hotel plunge pools
White weathered boats
Blue striped fluffy towels

Blue plastic coated sunbed cushions
White and sandy walk boards
Blue banded flagpole
White tell-tale bikini lines
Blue of the national flag
White louvred shutters
Blue forged iron gates
White foamy spume on the beach
Blue and moody music bar.

*Inspired by the vivid blue and white, seen both in the
Greek landscape and flag.*

Welcome Rain

Dry earth breathes again.

Damp leaves soak up welcome rain.

Gardeners will smile.

Autumn

Forage harvest boughs.

Colourful with'ring branches

Release, fall, repair.

Conkers

Smooth mahogany

Autumn treasure found, tempting

To hold, touch and keep.

Sunset

Day turns to peach dusk,

Radiant colours mute clouds.

Unique sunset sky.

Fabulous Sky

Opalescent crystals
Reflect pale rainbows
Across the twilight sky.
Soft, warm pastel colours
Tease us, as the icy winds
Cross bare fields and vale.
Nodding to father moon
On this solstice eve,
Mother of pearl clouds
As candy tulle high above,
Dance, welcoming
The longest night of the year.

Inspired by rare nacreous clouds. Known for the coloured light they reflect after sunset and before sunrise. Colours reminiscent of those reflected from a thin layer of oil on top of water, an effect known as iridescence.

After

After the clouds, maybe there comes rain.

After the rain, woohoo, a rainbow.

After the rainbow, welcome the sunshine.

After the sunshine, you can feel the warmth.

After the warmth, wow, admire the flowers.

After the flowers, pick out their heady scent.

After the memorable scent, remember my perfume.

After my perfume, you might miss my cool hand.

After my cool hand, there seems to be nothing…

After nothing, there is still, actually, our love.

Winter Togs

Winter hats and woollen gloves
Would keep us snug and warm,
But rarely can we match them up
Into pairs that should be worn.

They often sit alone in drawers
Throughout the other months,
To be tipped out and often found
With holes from hungry moths.

We turn ourselves into bulky folk
With garments in multi layers,
Our figures lost in thick winter togs,
We move like ice-hockey players.

Winter Walk

Breath mists on rosy cheeks,
Squinting against the low-slung sun.
Blessed to have a clear winter blue sky,
Briskly walking to warm ourselves.

Boots crunch through frosted leaves
Kicked into piles by wind or dogs.
Hands bound up in woolly gloves,
Friendship casually shared.
An avenue of stripped bare trees
Gives chill shade, our scarves pulled tight.

The only bright colours against the sleeping shrubs
Cheered to see the pavilion lights aglow.
A welcome hot drink beckons from the cosy café.
Time to chat of our plans for spring,
When days will be longer,
The sun higher and warmer,
Our moods and hearts much lighter.

Hygge

Shorter days, as chill air cools our brow.

Wind changes direction,

Strengthens, pitches as a storm blows in

With its uncontrollable energy.

Boughs sway, golden leaves fall in total disarray.

Walking briskly to heat our too cool blood,

Capture blue sky between clouds billowing overhead.

Deeply fill lungs with air so fresh and damp, it hurts.

Savour friendship together, holding hands and space.

Cast off cosy hats, coats, gloves and scarves.

The warming comforts of fire and flames beckon,

Drawing us closer, lighting up our smiles

Once again to be calm, soothed and rested.

Winter

Withdraw within — slow.

Allow quiet, calm restore.

Regroup, root deep, sleep.

Inspired by "Wintering" by Katherine May.

Wintering

I close the door now to the cold and dark.
To light the fire, I will need a fresh spark.
Reminds me of times, our minds and muscles tight,
We held each other warmly, close well into the night.

Flames now play in the hearth up the flue,
My mind keeps returning to thoughts of you.
Years made up of love, time now has passed,
We never knew that they would not last.

Winter evenings rake up fond memories of you.
No way could I forget those times for us two,
Holding our hearts in such a homely space,
It takes away my breath, fills me with grace.

A Christmas Eve Wish

If you're alone this Christmas, maybe feeling sad,

Perhaps you have a house full just driving you mad.

There are those who would keep asking Santa for

more,

But others go without as they really are poor.

In countries at war, they pray only for peace.

Too many stay out rough, wanting some quiet to sleep.

As Christmas Eve cools, darkness lit by moonlight,

And stars in their multitude come to shine out bright,

I wish for you all a day tomorrow of good cheer,

And trust that we'll all have a better new year.

Oh, Christmas Tree!

As soon as December begins, I stand up tall.
Each year I have grown from being quite small.
My branches are full of dusky cedar spines,
To attract those who choose these seasonal alpines.
But they walk past my place shaking heads saying,
"No,"
Without knowing why, just not my time to go.

Another is chosen, cut down in its prime.
Spread out limbs are now tied down tightly with twine.
Felled tree is then carried by road and by car,
Who knows where it ends up, whether near or far?
To be put up indoors, weights around its brown bark,
Adorned with tinsel and lights to glow in the dark.
All baubles and toys, gold coins, candy canes,
Hardly able to see the beautiful green spruce again.

A strong scent of pine released in the air.
Is it possible to give some water, please do care?
Wrapped presents are piled up underneath, looking
fancy.
There is a big party happening, what are its chances?
For the needles will fall all around as it cries,
Making everyone cross, they are like tears as it dies.

A day or few later, the tree now a stump
Is stripped then torn down, outside it is dumped.
Perhaps I shall hide in the field corner again,
Show off sparkly hoar frosts than have to endure pain?
If you wish to have a real spruce tree in your home,
Please consider a rental or one with roots in damp
loam.

A Tartan Toast

Take the sky blue so clear,
Pair it next to lavender and white.
For heather borders with summer clouds,
A rich weave; warm, close, soft.
Telling stories of clans through years,
A choice made consciously,
Marking a partnership,
Separate histories,
Interlocked lives.

The calm and generous rock
Blends with a flighty, airy lily.
Names chosen at birth,
North and south of a man-made border.
Tots poured of amber hue,
Rich in peat and mountain dew
To our overlapping futures,
Good health and fortune.

With My Blessing

I embrace you so closely, as I hold in all my tears.
Letting you go will never lessen my fears.
Gasping for air now, as I hug you so tight,
Unable to break bread with you - after tonight.

Forgive me for putting you on this strange train,
With others you don't know but are sharing your pain.
Wherever your journey goes, please write to me.
I will endeavour to stay where you've known me to be.

Treasure your case full of small mementoes;
Your hairbrush, my best shawl and some family photos.
Make the most of all hours travelling along distant
tracks.
Commit views to memory as I become part of your
past.

While you tend to your hair each morning and eve,
Remember I never, ever wanted you to leave.
My hope is that we will, in time, re-unite.
Take care, my dear daughter and with my blessing,
good night.

*Inspired by artwork "Mummy Don't Let Me Go - Despair
& Defiance" by Lynne Whitfield and refugee
memorabilia at The National Holocaust Centre.*

Come Home

Come home to me, my dear son,
Your many growing years are not done.
There is so much more
You are needed here for.
Come home to me, my dear son.

Come home to me, my lover,
Ourselves have only just discovered.
There is so much more
We have been planning for.
Come home to me, my lover.

Come home to me, my good friend,
Our land and peace you serve to defend.
There is so much more
Your whole life is meant for.
Come home to me, my good friend.

Come home to me, my hero,
Their vicious fight meant you had to go.
There is so much more
I now need you here for.
Come home to me, my hero.

Inspired by the young adults having to go to war.

Remember Me?

Remember me?
We hugged, I smiled, marched away proud.
So many Union Jacks waving high in the crowd.
A glorious cheer, hue and cry voiced aloud.

Remember me?
Your school pal, sibling, son or maybe good mate,
Last seen drinking down the noisy local on the estate.
Wishing I could be there, getting a round in, now it's too
late.

Remember me?
Your loved one sent off to such a strange, foreign
place.
Fighting daily for freedom, we all prayed for grace.
Battling across no man's land, there would be no trace.

Remember me?
Mind numb, knee-deep in mud, blooded khaki and
bone.
There's me composing letters for sending folks back
home.
So many lost but the rest feeling ultimately alone.

Remember me?

Your dear one, who gave their prime adult years to
serve
As private or officer, for the peace we all deserve.
Who knew of the ammo and bullets we'd need to
swerve?

Remember us?

We cannot come home, we gave more than we should,
Our hearts, our souls and finally, our blood.
They had to bury us out there, just as best they could.

Remember me!

Seen as a simple cross in a field, amongst rows of
many more
Stand tall at the cenotaph, poppies red, all adorned.
Who will ever understand what this cold stone
monument is even for?

Ribbons and Pins

A huge slab of stone stands there, for our freedom.
Your heart beats loudly, the rhythm of a military drum.
Uniforms and boots march, in time, past your place.
Salty tears form, start to roll down your face,
Remembering fondly whose medals you wear.
Life unfulfilled, ribbons and pins to bear
Close to your heart with that ancient photo.
Reliving each moment together; your loss of hope.

At the strike of the bell, slowly bow down your head.
Salutes from old comrades, stomach of lead.
Hold yourself up to the gaze of the crowd.
Your loved one, sacrificed in duty, who's so proud,
Is with you, behind you, in spirit and love.
Blood red poppies now presented, a pure white dove
Drops a feather before you, so you are aware,
You'll never be alone, I shall always be there.

How Many More Lives?

How many more lives

Will be lost in senseless war?

Misery; hearts break.

Inspired by the outbreak of yet another war.

Tears

Wiping dry my tears,
I am so much aware and realise
I cry not for the Queen,
Despite her constant presence
In my sixty-plus years.

No, I cry for all those
Whom no one will mourn;
The lonely,
Those living alone or
Whose friends have preceded and
Any family already passed.

There are no crowds to applaud,
The wake is silent as dawn.
Loyal pets once so beloved
Are now all left behind.

For these lost souls, I shed a tear
And light a candle
In my heart.

Dancing Seagulls

Bleak torrents of wintry rain darken the day,
Sluicing the road as we drive on our way.
Powerful gusts bend trees, nearly take control,
As we try to avoid floods in the road.

The sun tries its best to break through the gloom,
But multi-shades of heavy grey clouds loom.
Finding a place to sit, watch the sea, stay inside,
Seems a perfect way to pause, think and hide.

Brutal winds catch our breath, hurl like a swarm,
As we wrap up with woolly layers, hoping for warmth.
The boiling brown sea crashes onto the sands,
Our gloves gripped together, damp on our hands.

Dancing seagulls are a comic sight, that is true,
On the grassy cliff banks behind posh beach huts of
blue.
By the amusements many dog walkers, hardy souls,
smile.
We find a cosy cafe to just sit for a while.

We've come to say farewell to a very good friend.
His love for life and his family will continue, not end.
Dedicated to a friend and ex-colleague David Hudson.

Buzzards

Sun high, blue above
Clouds, like wing feathers, sweep by,
Catch plumes in bright rays.

Shadow cast below,
On fertile fields, abundant
Prey spotted, dive, live.

Black wings signal red.
Try undergrowth for safety,
Too slow to escape.

Lost Space

Lost inside these four walls,
Our own home has now
shrunk in around us,
Creating too tight a skin
Even to breathe.

Space, which always seemed
Plentiful, now develops and holds
An atmosphere too tense,
Choking the very life from all and
Everyone within.

Knots

Dreams come aplenty in the night,

Tying my mind up in ever-tightening knots.

How to stop them unravelling and thoughts escaping?

Perhaps a net, all holes, within my head,

Open to the fresh air and light,

Fashioned from knots, like a handkerchief, in the

corners

Will help me remember us tying the knot,

Deep and lovingly between our hearts?

Once, two ships, carrying hearts, knotted and coiled,

Sailed freely at many knots across the ocean,

Are now secured, by anchored rope knots.

A rug beneath my bed, created in knots of silk,

Keeps the rich pattern of our friendship grounded.

The boards beneath, full of knots and burrs,

Have the patina of aged polish and wear.

My soles reach down as I stir and stretch,

Knots loosen, freeing my spirit and soul.

Sun Rising

Bright sun rising east.

Blue sky expands, clouds disperse.

Breathe in your new day.

Flying High

Tension mounts in both my belly and the wire.
Taught muscles, gleaming wings, connected by a
chord,
Pulled into the sky and up, up into the wispy clouds.

Blue sky above, green woods and rich pastures below.
A smooth spiral takes me higher and higher,
Gaining altitude but losing clarity of all below.

Taken into the wind to best use nature's vast energy,
Released by a trigger, now soaring freely, like a raptor,
Swooping in a clean, lofty curve, observed from the
ground.

My view expands, admiring Wales and the Severn.
Seconds feel like minutes in this vacuum of reality.
Minutes of tightly managed falling towards the ground.
Flight of an eagle, but wings like light feathers
outstretched.

Practice makes possible, the gentle approach to land,
Safe on terra firma once again, with memories vivid of
Gliding from heaven to earth, quite magical.

Inspired by watching a glider in flight.

Friendship Bench

Come, why not sit by me?
I shall keep my distance
Until you feel comfortable.

We can just breathe and be,
Holding enough space,
Watching the world go by.
Listening to the birds sing,
Seeing the new grass so green,
Touching the painted wood beneath us,
Perhaps tasting that takeaway coffee
Still warm in your hand, through the plastic lid?

Taking time to reflect on our lives'
Ups and downs,
Just like a rollercoaster.

If you'd like to talk, then
I would be OK to listen.

Maybe, you'd listen to me…
Because I would like to talk,
Sometime.

Dusty

I put it to one side, just for a short while.

Now, as I come to tidy, there it is,

Covered with a fine layer of dust,

Gathered over years of work and family,

Virtually gasping for breath and light.

Why has it taken me so long?

Other parts of my life have superseded,

My own self confidence feels left on the shelf.

Now is the time to get back up and be strong.

I am me.

I am here.

I have gifts and talents to offer the world.

My time to dust is now.

The Emerging Man

The force is visible, visceral,
So very real.

Thrusting up and out
Towards liberty,
Away from cruel incarceration.

Once held in a cold, dark, brutal place,
The energy now unleashed,
Impossible to contain any longer,
Rises, fills the belly and explodes the lungs.

A matador with his past trailing as a cape behind,
Arms raised in defiance,
Poised,
Loins girded,
Is ready for the fight
Of his life.

*Inspired by "The Emerging Man" sculpture at the
National Holocaust Museum by Maurice Blik (b.1939),
held at Bergen-Belsen but liberated with his mother and
sister.*

Van Gogh

Picture this, my friend,

Stars bright on indigo sky,

Immersed in Vincent.

Ancient Parchments

Marks feather-inked onto rough textured surface,
Worked by candle or lamplight deep into the dark.

Meanings lost in the many centuries gone by.
Symbols designed timely to define.

Portray feelings, thoughts, dreams and deeds,
A far cry from animations, pixels and screens.

Emojis, now the current hieroglyphs
Describe life and experiences that
May defy future scribes.
No physical trace might be seen.

Kintsugi

It took only a second.
A lapse of concentration,
My mind on the day ahead, not the task in hand.
Falling, in slow motion, onto the cold tiles,
Clean but broken.

Large, sharp-edged chunks of my favourite bowl
Spread out beneath me.
Mornings of healthy oat breakfasts,
Warm, satisfying hearty lunch soups,
All vividly flashed before me.

Now I am piecing it back together
With a strong, magic glue.
Adding gold glitter to the mix,
Patience and mindful crafting,
Intense concentration in this task.

The joy to keep this beautiful thing,
With so much more to offer,
Now made glorious in its rebirth
Is very real and defined.

*Kintsugi = Japanese art of repairing pottery with gold,
so making it more valuable than the original item.*

The Stiperstones

Arthritic spine juts and erupts heavenward.

Through soft, mossy earth,

Holding stark court in the landscape,

Stripped back,

Raw,

Bleached.

All-encompassing points around,

Skylarks cry in the breeze.

Crazy Paving

The pattern suggests flustered, hurried movement.
An impromptu canvas,
Uneven, horizontal.
Unexpected diagonals cross
Here, go there.

After an accidental, feline mishap,
Chaos, mayhem, heard loud in the night.
Fur and paws now clogged with Vanilla Ice,
Unwitting artists with their bristle brushes.

The massive spillage now left to us
To scrub clean.

Festival Bubbles

Iridescent, pearly globes rise into the air,

Floating up above the square.

Multitudes of colours,

Mobile rainbows touching the blue sky.

Cheering the crowds,

Bringing wide smiles;

Children at heart, everyone.

A delight in simplicity,

Surely there is no one

Who does not like bubbles?

New Shoes

Crafted soft, kid leather,

Strong but supple around my foot.

One shiny buckle secures the strap.

The low kitten heel behind a flexible sole,

Modern but modest.

A perfect fit.

I shall take these.

Croeso

Welcome to the beginning of this brand-new day.

Starting out on a wonderful life,

Strive and excel.

There will be no rival to all your charm.

Be bold, be bright, be true.

Hold close your dreams within your heart.

Croeso, bienvenue, welcome.

For Emlyn Viorel Bartle-Brestin b. 01/07/22.

Truth

Feeling in your gut,
You know it to be true.
The doubt has lifted and the light shines.

Others around you are unaware
That you have found the truth
Deep inside.

Follow your path to your destiny.
Be alert to those people who might divert you
And things that may distract.

Keep true to your own truth.

Sensory Memory

I could walk blindfold through the open door,
Knowing instantly it is a library or bookstore.

An antiquarian's delight,
Full of books exuding tell-tale aroma of carbon black
ink,
Set out on parchment and paper.

Glue from animal bones now strong, turned acrid.
Tanned leather, hammered thin, embossed with pure
gold.

Musty volumes, stacked high all around
Fill the air with ages of words and vast wisdom.

Stories, facts, picture, maps and poems
Restrained within sturdy racks.
Catalogued, bookended, contained.

Senses alert, never to forget,
Dust motes quiver.

Drive

Sometimes in the fast lane, often the slow,
But life pushes us ever forward, even so.

The U-turns and roundabouts on decisions we make,
Give us the colour and depth to which road we might
take.

There are limits in speed and diversions to endure.
Events can be closed down, we know for sure.

We often have to stop, take a breath and give way
For thoughts and desires to come along, who can say?

There is only one way to really prosper and thrive,
And that is getting right out there and finding your drive.

Seaside Reunion

Waves crashing in on the evening tide,

Brown, surging, over the prom,

High, powerful, boiling mad,

Spewing dead weed, gravel and sand.

Full moon, through sparse front clouds,

Silver, lighting up ruthless white tops.

Nature uncontrolled, merciless.

Memories lurching from the deep.

Stories from years, long passed.

Youth, blunder and heartbreaks re-aired.

Drinks loosening tongues,

Warming up lost songs,

Lubricating limbs unused to dance.

Faces, now wisdom, life and laughter grained,

Heads nodding faint recognition.

Lean in close to hug and air-kiss anew.

So many with hair receded or greyed,

Figures somewhat shifted after four decades.

Holding loose catch-up conversations
Loudly, above seventies disco hits.
So many together but so many missing,
We raise a toast to absent friends.
How long until the golden one?

Inspired by my school reunion.

Smile

Lips hold tight a smile.

Dark lens too close, in my face.

Do I know my place?

Weathered

Age sits quietly
In the lines by your eyes.

Wisdom, laughter,
Just many years passed.

So much emotion,
So many tears,
So many smiles.

Sun, rain, wind and frost
Have bleached your skin.

Age is not just about the number of years,
Age is all about your experience in those years.

Youngsters may only see the lines,
You have the learning to decipher their questions.

The strength and integrity built to withstand
Close inspection, interrogation and comment.

Respond with humility, love and grace.

Honour your lines.

Blue

Into the deep blue,

I see my own reflection.

Your eyes hold my soul.

Tend

Take care of the little things

Every being is here for a reason

No act of kindness is unseen

Dedicate your life to love of life

Stone in my Pocket

How long have you been there,
Deep within my pocket,
Warmed and familiar?

A touchstone, a friend.

Textured and engrained
With many thoughts, personal wishes
Rubbed in with my thumb.

It is always calming to feel
Your flat heart shape there.

Did I save you from the sea,
As mean tide moved the shingle,
Or perhaps from a brook
Rippling down a hillside?

You will never be a skimmer,
Lost kissing some lapping, lakeside water,
Or a window breaker -
No venom contained therein.

I could not leave you on a hilltop cairn,
I am too fond of you.
Familiar company on life's ventures.

I shall just have to leave
My words on stony ground.

Fill Up with Love

Sweet raindrops will absolutely fall

From moody clouds high above,

To fill up fast rivers and streams,

Refresh thoughts, help you recall dreams.

Your salty tears from tired eyes may flow;

Evidence of many joys, mighty sorrows,

Filling up oceans, deep and blue;

Mean tides pulled in-out by the moon.

A vast universe of possibilities

Reveals your path written in the stars.

Welcome your new energy to explore

The waiting, breathing world out there.

Fill up your heart with warm, true love;

Your open mind with wisdom and truth.

Life's journey will reward you plenty,

With many gifts more precious than gold.

Dedicated to Freya Adele Lewis b.22/04/24

Mothers' Love

Many have known or know our mothers.

Everyday, seemingly there for everything;

We can visualise her face, hear her voice.

Do we instinctively look for guidance to

Help us on our way? Maybe.

Her wisdom in reckoning, judging,

Supporting but secretly dreaming.

Loving and caring, thinking of

Opportunities she may never have had.

Virtually living, breathing through us;

Endeavouring to let her offspring fly.

We are the fortunate ones,

Others sadly, have or cannot.

Loving Hands

Take hold,
Don't let go.

Your hand is so warm and soft,
Nails neat, filed and natural.

Reach out,
Touch the skin, so fair.

A face with few wrinkles,
By true, bright blue eyes.

Your fingers curl around,
Treasuring the heart within,
Full of love, kindness, humanity.

Take hold,
Do not fear the load.
It is true love right there,
Even if the fingers are cold.

Take care, my love,
Of your hands so open;
A haven between palms.

Be true to yourself,
Aim to be kind.

Give to your own heart
All that you give to mine.

Dedicated to Alex

89

Reviews

Sue McFarlane's newest poetry collection, *Words on Stony Ground*, ties the reader to "this moment now". Her gentle words explore days of life, love and loss, as she touches on simple truths to reveal to us the comfort of the forgotten treasure in the pocket, the "welcome to the beginning of this brand new day". While dancing lightly between various poetic forms, she visits nature, seasons, remembrance, celebration and always, hope. Her passion for finding words and her world of imagery encourage the reader to enjoy life. These poems offer roses, optimism and art that all glimmer with colour and peace. These poems repair our injuries with the Japanese art of Kintsugi, joining fissures with gold. These poems offer worthy friendship to the reader, admonishing "Be bold, be bright, be true".

I thank Sue for this peace-making collection that invites us to a moment for ourselves, where we may "Sit quietly / Breathe deeply / Be still".

- *Laura Grevel*
- Laura Grevel, from Texas, has lived in Europe for 23 years. She is a performance poet, fiction writer & blogger. Her poetry is eclectic, tackling the immigrant experience, politics, storytelling & nature. Laura's work is published in many anthologies, podcasts & online publications.

Words on Stony Ground is a gentle, heartfelt collection of poems, guiding the reader through the ups and downs of this ridiculous and joyful thing we call life. Sue's poetry explores nature, interpersonal relationships, spirituality, and the rich emotional inner monologue we all carry.

- *Leanne Moden*

- Leanne Moden is a poet, performer & writer, based in Nottingham. She runs events, projects & workshops all over the county, bringing the creative side out in so many people. Her many subjects include womanhood & belonging. Leanne is well recognised, has lots of her work published & is much featured online.

Index

About the Author

After retiring from her own complementary therapies practice of over 20 years, Sue McFarlane has really found her creative voice and explores many topics within this work. Born in East Yorkshire, now living in Nottinghamshire with her husband and three rescue cats, Sue enjoys rambling in the countryside, exploring nature, cooking and gardening.

Sue's other books

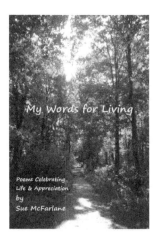 

www.green-cat.shop/sue-mcfarlane

For more information about our books, or if you would like to discuss publishing, please visit www.green-cat.shop

Green Cat Books